PICNIC
RECIPES

compiled by
Carol Wilson

*with charming studies
of children at play*

SALMON

Index

Cover pictures *front:* Harvesters at Lunch *by A. W. Weedon*
back: Lilacs *by Thomas James Lloyd*   *title page*: The Stile *by Helen Allingham*

Printed and Published by J. Salmon Ltd., Sevenoaks, England © Copyright

Picnic Pie

An excellent pie that is always a favourite for a summer picnic.

12 oz shortcrust pastry   **Salt and pepper**
8 oz bacon, chopped   **1 oz butter**
6 large eggs

Set oven to 400°F or Mark 6. Roll out just over half the pastry and line a 9 inch pie dish or deep flan tin. Melt the butter in a frying pan and cook the bacon gently until just coloured. Drain well and arrange on the base of the pastry. Break the eggs on to the bacon, placing 5 around the edge and 1 in the centre. Tilt the dish so that the whites meet. Add a sprinkling of salt (omit this if the bacon is salty) and pepper. Roll out the remaining pastry and cover the pie, sealing the edges well. Glaze with beaten egg or milk and bake for 25 minutes then reduce the heat to 325°F or Mark 3 and bake for another 15 minutes. Serve cold cut into slices.

Waiting for a Bite *by Fanny Mary Minns*

Walnut Bread

This bread is delicious sliced and buttered and eaten with cheese.

1 lb flour
9 oz molasses or dark soft brown sugar
1/2 teaspoon ground cinnamon
Pinch of ground cloves

1 teaspoon baking powder
1/2 teaspoon salt
5 oz walnuts, cut in half or chopped
2 eggs, beaten

1/2-3/4 pint milk

Set oven to 350°F or Mark 4. Grease and line a 2 lb loaf tin. Sift the flour, baking powder, cinnamon and cloves into a large mixing bowl, then sift in the molasses sugar. Stir in the salt and the walnuts, then beat in the eggs. Slowly pour in the milk, beating all the time until the mixture is like a paste and is hard to beat. Put the mixture into the tin and cook for about 45 to 60 minutes until the loaf is cooked through and a skewer inserted comes out clean. Let the loaf cool in the tin for a few minutes then turn out on to a wire rack to become cold.

Herb Paté

Serve this sliced with fresh crusty bread.

10 oz cooked or frozen spinach	**Grated nutmeg**
1 lb lean pork, minced	**Salt and pepper**
4 oz cooked bacon, chopped	**1 egg**
1 small onion, chopped finely	**4 rashers streaky bacon**

2 tablespoons mixed fresh herbs, e.g. thyme, basin, parsley, sage, rosemary

Set oven to 350°F or Mark 4. Cook sufficient fresh spinach to produce 10 oz (about 1½ lb leaves) or use frozen, thawed, then press and drain well and pat with kitchen paper until very dry. Chop the spinach and place in a mixing bowl with the rest of the ingredients, except the bacon rashers and mix very well to combine. Press the mixture into a 2 lb loaf tin or a 1½ pint dish and cover with the bacon rashers. Cover with foil and stand in a roasting tin. Pour in hot water to come half way up the sides of the tin or dish. Place in the oven and cook for about 1 hour until cooked through. Remove from the oven and place a heavy weight on top. When cool, chill overnight in the refrigerator, still with the weight on top; this makes it easier to slice.

Chilled Cucumber Soup

Very refreshing on a hot summer day.

2 large cucumbers	1 small onion, halved
2 oz butter	1 bay leaf
½ teaspoon granulated sugar	1 oz flour
Salt and pepper	15 fl oz vegetable or chicken stock
10 fl oz milk	5 fl oz single cream

Peel the cucumbers, cut in half lengthways and scoop out the seeds. Chop the flesh and blanch in boiling water for 2 minutes; this preserves the green colour. Melt half the butter in a pan and add the cucumber, sugar and salt and pepper to taste. Cover and cook gently for about 15 minutes until soft. Heat the milk with the onion halves and bay leaf in another pan. Bring just to boiling point, then remove from the heat, cover and leave to stand for at least 10 minutes. Melt the remaining butter in a pan over a low heat and stir in the flour. Cook for 1 minute. Gradually add the milk (discard the onion and bay leaf) stirring constantly to make a thick smooth sauce. Add this to the cucumbers with the stock and cook over a low heat for 15 minutes. Purée the mixture in a food processor or blender or push through a sieve. Return the soup to the rinsed pan and stir in the cream. Check the seasoning and leave until cold. Chill in the refrigerator until needed.

Chicken Parcels

The light, fresh taste of the apple stuffing makes these chicken pasties moist and appetising.

2 chicken breasts	**2 oz fresh breadcrumbs**
2 oz butter	**Grated rind of $\frac{1}{2}$ lemon**
1 onion, peeled and	**Salt and black pepper**
finely chopped	**A little beaten egg to glaze**
1 small eating apple (e.g. Cox)	**8oz to 12oz shortcrust pastry depending**
peeled, cored and finely chopped	**on the size of the chicken breasts**

Set oven to 400°F or Mark 6. Grease a baking tray. Cut a slit in the side of each breast to form a pocket. Melt 1 oz of the butter in a frying pan and lightly fry the breasts on both sides for about one minute to seal. Mix the onion and apple together. Melt the remaining butter in a saucepan and add the onion mixture. Cover and cook over a very low heat until the onion and apple are soft. Mix together the onion mixture, breadcrumbs, lemon rind and seasoning, then bind with the beaten egg. Stuff the pockets in the chicken breasts with the mixture. Roll out the pastry on a lightly floured surface. Divide in half and wrap up the breasts to form parcels, sealing well. Decorate with trimmings. Brush with milk or beaten egg to glaze and place on the baking tray. Cook for about 30 minutes or until the pastry is golden brown. Transfer to a wire rack to cool and serve cold.

The Stick Fire *by Kate Greenaway*

Cheddar Cheese Straws

These simple-to-make savoury straws bring a touch of party atmosphere to picnic fare.

4 oz flour	**2 oz butter, softened**
Pinch of salt	**2 oz strong Cheddar cheese, finely grated**
$^1/_2$ teaspoon dry mustard powder	**1 egg, beaten**

Set oven to 400°F or Mark 6. Lightly flour a baking tray. Place the flour, salt and mustard powder into a bowl. Rub in the butter until the mixture resembles breadcrumbs. Stir in the cheese and add enough egg to form a firm dough. Turn out on to a lightly floured surface and knead lightly until smooth. Roll out to a rectangle $^1/_4$ inch thick and cut into strips 3 inches by $^1/_2$ inch. Place on the baking tray and cook for 10 to 15 minutes until pale golden in colour. Transfer carefully to a wire rack to cool and then store in an airtight tin.

Chocolate Coconut Crunch

These are so easy to prepare that children will enjoy making them.

6 oz self-raising flour	**5 oz butter, softened**
Pinch of salt	**3 oz caster sugar**
1 tablespoon cocoa powder	**4 oz desiccated coconut**
	2 oz plain or milk chocolate

Set oven to 285ºF or Mark 1. Butter a 12 x 8 inches Swiss Roll tin. Sift the flour, salt and cocoa powder into a mixing bowl. Rub in the butter until the mixture resembles breadcrumbs. Stir in the sugar and coconut. Knead lightly then press into the buttered tin. Bake for 30 minutes. Leave to cool in the tin. Melt the chocolate in a bowl placed in hot water and spread it over the top of the cooled crunch, using a knife warmed in hot water. Finally, cut into bars or squares.

The Clothes Basket *by Helen Allingham*

Walnut & Honey Tart

A sweet crunchy treat with orange flavoured pastry.

6 oz flour	4 tablespoons honey
Pinch of salt	3 oz fresh wholemeal breadcrumbs
3 oz butter, softened	3 tablespoons dark muscovado sugar
Grated rind and juice of	3 eggs
1 large orange	4 oz walnuts, chopped roughly

Set oven to 400ªF or Mark 6. Grease an 8 inch flan tin. Sift the flour and salt into a mixing bowl and rub in the butter until the mixture resembles breadcrumbs. Stir in the orange rind and enough juice to form a soft dough. Roll out the dough on a lightly floured surface and use to line the base and sides of the tin. Bake blind for 10 to 15 minutes. Mix together in a bowl the honey, breadcrumbs and sugar, then gradually beat in the eggs and any remaining orange juice. Scatter the walnuts over the base of the pastry case and pour over the filling. Bake for 20 to 25 minutes until cooked through. If the tart is browning too fast during the cooking time, cover with kitchen foil. Cool in the tin, then finish cooling on a wire rack.

Savoury Pinwheels

A tasty snack made with that old favourite, Marmite.

8 oz shortcrust pastry   4 teaspoons Marmite
3 oz Cheddar cheese, grated

Set oven to 400ºF or Mark 6. Grease a baking sheet. Roll out the pastry on a lightly floured surface to a rectangle about 8 x 10 inches and trim the edges. Spread with Marmite to within $1/2$ inch of the edges and sprinkle with the cheese. Dampen the edges and roll up like a Swiss roll. Cut into slices about $1/4$ inch thick and place the slices on their sides on the baking tray. Bake for 10 to 15 minutes until bubbling, then remove from the oven and transfer to a wire rack to cool.

Meatballs with Dipping Sauce

These fruity, lightly spiced meatballs can be made with minced lamb if preferred.

9 oz no-soak apricots, chopped finely	**Salt and pepper**
1½ lb minced beef	**2 tablespoons oil**
2 garlic cloves, chopped finely	**1 tablespoon honey**
1 teaspoon ground cinnamon	**1 tablespoon white wine vinegar**
2 tablespoons tomato purée	

Mix together the apricots, beef, garlic, cinnamon and seasoning and roll into small balls with wet hands. Heat the oil in a frying pan and fry the meatballs for about 15 minutes over a medium heat, turning them around until browned on all sides. Remove from the pan and drain the meatballs on kitchen paper. Pour off the fat from the pan, reserving the juices. Add the honey, vinegar and tomato purée to the pan with 5 to 6 tablespoons water and cook gently until the glaze is thickened and glossy. Place the meatballs in a plastic box and pack the sauce separately. Cover when cold and keep in the refrigerator until needed.

Apricot & Cherry Rock Buns

There is nothing rock-like in the texture of these tempting little cakes! Rosewater imparts a lovely flavour.

3 oz butter, softened	2 oz glacé cherries, quartered or chopped
3 oz caster sugar	5 oz flour
3 oz ground almonds	2 eggs, beaten
2 oz no-soak apricots, chopped	1 teaspoon rose water (optional)

Beaten egg to glaze

Set oven to 425°F or Mark 7. Grease a baking tray. Cream together the butter and sugar in a mixing bowl until light and creamy. Add the ground almonds, apricots and cherries then stir in the flour with the eggs and rose water (if used). Mix to a stiff dough and place small mounds of the mixture on the baking tray. Glaze the buns with a little beaten egg and bake for 12 to 15 minutes. Transfer to a wire rack to cool.

The Primrose Gatherers *by Birket Foster*

Carrot and Raisin Salad

This salad can be made ahead of time and kept in an airtight container in the refrigerator.

1 lb carrots, peeled   8 oz raisins (Muscatel or Lexia are the best)
4 oz walnuts, halved   Grated zest and juice of 1 orange

Grate the carrots coarsely and mix with the raisins and walnuts. Add the orange juice and zest and stir well.

Orange and Rice Salad

A colourful tasty salad that is perfect for a summer picnic.

4 oz long grain white rice   1 orange   4 fl oz olive oil
2 tablespoons white wine vinegar   1 teaspoon granulated sugar
1 tablespoon parsley   Salt and pepper   1 stick celery, diced
6 spring onions, chopped   3 oz raisins   2 tablespoons flaked almonds

Wash the rice and cook in boiling salted water until tender; about 8 to 10 minutes. Meanwhile grate the zest from the orange and mix with the oil, vinegar, sugar, parsley and seasoning to taste. Drain the rice and while still warm stir in the oil dressing. Leave to cool then add the celery, spring onions, raisins and almonds. Remove the pith from the orange and divide the flesh into segments. Add to the rice and put into an airtight container and chill in the refrigerator until needed.

Scotch Egg

The ubiquitous Scotch Egg makes an excellent and ever popular stand-by for picnic or packed luncheon fare.

12 oz pork sausagemeat	1 oz flour, seasoned with salt and pepper
2 teaspoons parsley, finely chopped	1 egg, beaten
4 eggs	4 oz dried breadcrumbs

Vegetable oil for deep frying

Boil the eggs for 10 minutes. Cool and remove the shells. Place the sausagemeat in bowl, add the chopped parsley and mix well; hands are best. Coat the eggs with the seasoned flour and cover completely with a layer of sausagemeat; wet hands will help to mould it evenly. Dip each coated egg into the beaten egg and roll in the breadcrumbs. Fry in deep fat until golden brown. Drain well on kitchen paper and allow to get cold.

Brother and Sister *by Kate Greenaway*

Fruity Flapjacks

These little biscuits are very more-ish and, as they are packed full of healthy ingredients, they are healthy too!

2 oz walnuts	**3 bananas**
2 oz no-soak apricots	**2 tablespoons light muscovado sugar**
2 oz glacé cherries	**6 oz porridge oats**
1 oz currants (optional)	**1 oz desiccated coconut**

3 fl oz sunflower oil

Set oven to 350°F or Mark 4. Line a baking sheet with non-stick baking paper. Chop roughly the walnuts, apricots and glacé cherries. Mash the bananas with a fork. Put all the ingredients in to a large mixing bowl and mix together well. Drop spoonfuls of the mixture on to the lined baking sheet and flatten the top of each with a fork. Bake for about 20 minutes until golden brown. Cool on the tray for 5 minutes then transfer the biscuits to a wire rack to cool. When the flapjacks are completely cold, store in an airtight tin.

Little Mutton Pies

These individual, luxury pies are made to a 19th century recipe.

¹/₄ **pint red wine**	**1 teaspoon chopped fresh thyme**
¹/₂ **pint lamb stock**	**1 teaspoon chopped fresh parsley**
12 oz lean lamb, finely chopped	**Salt and black pepper**
1 onion, peeled and finely chopped	**1 lb prepared puff pastry**
8 oz mushrooms, finely chopped	**Beaten egg for glazing.**

Boil the wine in a large saucepan until it is reduced by one third, then stir in the stock. Add the lamb, onion, mushrooms, herbs and seasoning, bring to the boil then simmer for 30 minutes. Strain off the gravy and reserve and leave the meat mixture to get cold. Set oven to 375ºF or Mark 5. Roll out the pastry on a lightly floured surface and use to line 8 small greased ramekin dishes, reserving nearly half the pastry for the lids. Divide the meat mixture evenly between the pies. Skim any fat from the top of the gravy and put 1 dessertspoonful into each pie. Dampen the lids, place on the pies, crimp the edges and make a steam hole in the centre of each. Brush well with beaten egg. Bake for 35 to 40 minutes or until the pastry is crisp and golden. Very carefully remove the pies from the dishes and place on a wire rack. Heat the remaining gravy and pour a little into each pie through the steam hole. Serve cold with pickles.

American Corn Bread

Crisp outside and soft and moist inside, this bread is delicious when eaten with anything from jam to salad.

6 oz cornmeal	**1 teaspoon salt**
8 oz flour	**1 tablespoon granulated sugar**
2 teaspoons baking powder	**3 oz butter, softened**

Just over ¾ pint milk

Set oven to 350ºF or Mark 4. Grease a 10 x 8 inch baking tin or a 1 lb loaf tin. Put the cornmeal, flour, baking powder, salt and sugar into a large mixing bowl. Stir the ingredients together, then rub in the butter until the mixture resembles breadcrumbs. Make a hollow in the middle and gradually pour in the milk, stirring all the time, until a thick batter forms. Pour the mixture into the tin and bake for about 30 minutes until golden brown and cooked through, when a skewer inserted comes out clean. Turn out on to a wire rack to cool.

Picnic Pasty

Corned beef forms the basis of this large, flat pasty which can be cut up into squares or slices to suite individual appetites.

12 oz shortcrust pastry
1 large onion, peeled and finely chopped
1 large potato, peeled and diced
1 large carrot, peeled and diced
4 oz runner beans or celery, chopped
8 oz corned beef, chopped
Seasoning to taste
2 tablespoons gravy
Pinch of mixed herbs

Set oven to 400°F or Mark 6. Grease a 10 x 12 inch shallow baking tin. Place the onion, potato, carrot and beans or celery in a saucepan. Cover with boiling water and cook for 5 minutes. Meanwhile, roll out the pastry on a lightly floured surface and line the base and sides of the tin with a little more than half the pastry. Drain the vegetables, add the seasoning, herbs, corned beef and gravy and mix well. Cover the pastry with the filling, brush the edges with water and cover with another layer of pastry. Pinch and seal the edges. Brush the top with milk and bake for 40 minutes until golden. Eat cold, cut into squares or slices.

The Stepping Stones *by Henry Jutsam*

Apple & Raisin Pie

The rich spicy pastry for this pie is just as tasty as the fruity filling.

12 oz flour	3 oz light muscovado sugar
1 teaspoon ground cinnamon	1 egg, beaten
6 oz cold butter, diced	4 fl oz milk

FILLING: 1 lb cooking apples, peeled, cored and thinly sliced

1 tablespoon lemon juice	2 oz raisins
2 oz light muscovado sugar	Caster sugar for sprinkling

Set oven to 350°F or Mark 4. Grease a baking sheet. Sift the flour and cinnamon into a bowl and rub in the butter until the mixture resembles breadcrumbs. Stir in the sugar, followed by the egg and milk and mix to a soft dough. Turn out on to a floured surface and knead lightly. Roll out half the pastry into a 9 inch round and place on the baking sheet. Combine together all the filling ingredients. Cover the pastry with the filling, leaving a margin of $1/2$ inch round the edges. Dampen the edges of the pastry. Roll out the rest of the pastry to another 9 inch round. Cover the pie with the pastry round and pinch together to seal. Bake for 40 to 45 minutes until the pastry is golden brown. Sprinkle with caster sugar while hot and then allow to cool.

Butter Biscuits

Melt-in-the mouth biscuits with a rich buttery flavour.

7 oz butter, softened   **3 fl oz sweet sherry**
2½ oz caster sugar   **14 oz flour**

Set oven to 350ºF or Mark 4. Grease a baking sheet. Cream the butter and sugar in a bowl until light, then gradually beat in the sherry, a little at a time. Add the flour gradually until the mixture forms a soft dough. Roll out to ½ inch thickness (try not to handle the dough too much or it will become greasy) on a lightly floured surface and cut into rounds. Place on the baking sheet and bake for 15 to 20 minutes. Cool on the tray (the biscuits will crisp up as they cool) for a few minutes then carefully transfer to a wire rack to finish cooling.

On the Sands *by Helen Allingham*

Fresh Cherry Cake

A superb cake made with fresh cherries which give it a delightful flavour.

5 oz butter, softened	**2 large eggs, beaten**
5 oz ground almonds	**4 fl oz milk**
9 oz self-raising flour	**10 oz fresh cherries, stoned**
5 oz caster sugar	**1 oz flaked almonds**

Set oven to 350ºF or Mark 4. Grease and line a deep, 8 inch round cake tin. Put the flour into a mixing bowl and rub in the butter until the mixture resembles breadcrumbs. Stir in the ground almonds and sugar, then add the eggs, milk and cherries. Mix until combined, but do not over mix. Spoon into the cake tin and smooth the top. Scatter the flaked almonds over the top and bake for about 1 hour 10 minutes until the cake is golden and firm to the touch and a skewer inserted comes out clean. Leave in the tin for 10 minutes then turn out on to a wire rack to cool.

Walnut and Cinnamon Muffins

These American style muffins are light and airy and they are delicious.

5 oz flour	**1¹/₂ oz caster sugar**
¹/₂ tablespoon baking powder	**4 fl oz milk**
Pinch of salt	**2 oz butter, melted**
1 egg	**2 oz walnuts, chopped**

2 teaspoons ground cinnamon

TOPPING:

1 tablespoon Demerara sugar   **2 oz walnuts, finely chopped**

Set oven to 400°F or Mark 6. Grease 6 deep muffin tins or Yorkshire pudding tins. Sift the flour, baking powder and salt into a large mixing bowl. Combine the egg, sugar, milk and butter and stir quickly into the dry ingredients with the walnuts and cinnamon. Do not over beat the mixture and ignore any streaks of flour; the uneven appearance ensures the muffins will be light. Spoon into the muffin tins and sprinkle each with chopped walnuts and Demerara sugar. Bake for 30 minutes until well risen and golden brown. Cool in the tins for 5 minutes and then transfer to a wire rack to cool.

Picnic Omelette

A thick, cold omelette that looks impressive cut into wedges accompanied
by a crisp green salad.

1 lb new potatoes, scrubbed	**1 red pepper, chopped**
5 tablespoons oil	**8 oz cooked or frozen spinach**
1 onion, chopped	**6 eggs**

Salt and pepper

Cook the potatoes in boiling salted water until tender. Cool, then slice thickly. Cook the onion and pepper in the oil in a frying pan for 5 minutes then add the potatoes and cook until lightly browned. Cook sufficient fresh spinach to produce 8 oz (about 1¹/₄ lb leaves) or use frozen, thawed, then press and drain well. Stir the spinach into the pan and cook for 1 minute. Whisk together the eggs and seasoning and pour into the pan, stirring. Cook gently for 10 minutes until set. Place the pan under a hot grill for a few minutes until the top is browned. Stand for 10 minutes then turn out on to a plate and leave to cool. Serve cold, cut into wedges.

Pineapple and Coconut Teabread

Moist and fruity, this light teabread is sure to be a favourite.

14 oz tin pineapple pieces, well drained	2 medium eggs
2 oz glacé cherries, quartered	4 oz flour
4 oz butter, softened	2 teaspoons baking powder
4 oz soft brown sugar	3 oz desiccated coconut

Set oven to 350ºF or Mark 4. Grease and line a 2 lb loaf tin. Put all the ingredients into a large mixing bowl and beat well with a wooden spoon for 3 minutes or with an electric mixer for 1 minute. Spoon into the tin and smooth the top. Bake for 1 to 1½ hours until cooked through when a skewer inserted comes out clean. Cool in the tin for 10 minutes, then turn out on to a wire rack to finish cooling.

The Garden Seat *by Kate Greenaway*

Sticky Chicken Pieces

Delectably sticky, so be sure to take lots of napkins for mopping up.

12 chicken thighs
5 oz dark soft brown sugar
2 fl oz lemon juice

3 tablespoons sherry or ginger wine
2 cloves garlic
2 tablespoons soy sauce

Ground white pepper to taste.

Put all the ingredients except the chicken into a pan over a low heat and stir until the sugar has dissolved completely. Increase the heat and bring to the boil, then cook for 2 to 3 minutes. Remove from the heat. Put the chicken thighs into a large dish and pour over the sauce. Cover and leave to stand for a few hours. In due course, set oven to 400ºF or Mark 6. Remove the chicken pieces from the marinade and place them in a roasting tin. Cook for 10 minutes, then baste with a little more sauce, just enough to make the chicken pieces sticky. Cook for another 15 to 20 minutes until cooked. Place the chicken pieces under a hot grill for a few minutes to crisp slightly. Leave to cool and serve cold.

Sausage Plait

A more decorative way than sausage rolls of presenting sausagemeat wrapped in pastry.

8 oz shortcrust pastry

FILLING

8 oz sausagemeat	**2 oz mushrooms, chopped**
2 tomatoes, chopped	**Pinch of mixed herbs**
1 small onion, peeled and chopped	**Salt and pepper**

Beaten egg to glaze

Set oven to 400°F or Mark 6. Grease a baking tray. Chop the tomatoes, onion and mushrooms and mix in a bowl with the sausagemeat and the herbs. Roll out the pastry on a floured surface to a rectangle about 12 inches by 9 inches and place on the baking tray. Arrange the filling down the centre of the pastry. Cut the pastry down each side of the filling into $1/2$ inch strips at an angle. Fold the pastry strips, alternately, over the mixture to look like a plait. Brush with beaten egg and bake for 30 to 35 minutes. Transfer to a wire rack to cool and eat cold.

In a Summer Garden *by Helen Allingham*

Butter Tarts

These deliciously creamy fruit tartlets make a real treat for any picnic spread.

8 oz prepared shortcrust pastry	**1 egg, beaten**
3 oz butter	**A few drops vanilla essence**
6 oz soft brown sugar	**2 tablespoons single cream**
4 oz raisins or sultanas	**A little milk, optional**

Set oven to 350ªF or Mark 4. Roll out the pastry on a lightly floured surface and use to line 12 to 16 lightly greased tartlet tins. Melt the butter in a saucepan, stir in the remaining ingredients and spoon into the pastry cases, brushing the pastry edges with a little milk, if desired. Bake for 20 to 25 minutes or until golden. Remove from the tins and cool on a wire rack.

Iced Tea Punch

Cooling and refreshing on a hot day, this is much nicer than sweet, fizzy drinks.

6 Earl Grey teabags   3 tablespoons caster sugar   2 inch piece cinnamon stick
2 pints boiling water   Juice of 2 oranges   Juice of 1 lemon

Put the teabags, sugar and cinnamon stick into a large jug and pour on the boiling water. Leave to infuse for 5 to 10 minutes then strain and add the fruit juices. Allow to cool then chill in the refrigerator before transferring to a vacuum flask.

Fresh Potato Crisps

These are very easy and economical to make and taste much nicer than commercially produced crisps.

4 medium size, floury potatoes   Oil for deep frying   Salt

Peel the potatoes and cut into wafer thin slices. Put the slices into a large bowl of cold water and swirl them around to remove the starch. Dry the slices in a tea towel. Heat the oil to 190ºC/375ºF in a deep pan and fry the potato slices in small batches until golden and crisp. Drain on absorbent kitchen paper and sprinkle with salt. When cold keep in an airtight tin.

Raspberry Fizz

This is a delicious cooling drink which is packed with vitamin C.

1 lb fresh raspberries   3 oz caster sugar
1 pint carbonated mineral water (or sparkling white wine for grown-ups)

Blend the raspberries and sugar together in a blender or food processor to make a purée. Sieve the purée to remove the seeds and pour into a large jug. Add the water or sparkling wine and pour into a chilled vacuum flask.

Lemon Mint Coolade

Lemon and mint are a refreshing combination and make a cooling picnic drink.

1 pint fizzy lemonade, chilled   4 slices lemon
1 pint apple juice, chilled   8 sprigs fresh mint

In a large jug, mix together the lemonade and apple juice with the sliced lemon. Pour into a chilled vacuum flask if required. Lightly crush the mint leaves to release the flavour, put a sprig of mint in each glass and pour in the drink.

Chocolate Fudge Flan

A rich, sweet nutty fudge filling covered with chocolate. Serve in small slices.

6 oz digestive biscuits, crushed   **2 oz butter**

FILLING:

10 oz light muscovado sugar   **5 fl oz water**

2 oz butter   **2 oz hazelnuts, chopped**

5 fl oz double cream   **2 oz plain chocolate**

Melt the butter and mix with the biscuit crumbs. Press into the base and sides of a greased 8 inch flan tin or dish and chill until needed. Put the sugar and water into a pan and heat gently until the sugar has dissolved. Bring to the boil and simmer without stirring until the mixture is a straw coloured caramel. Remove from the heat and stir in the butter, hazelnuts and all but one dessertspoon of the cream. Return to the heat and bring to the boil. Simmer for 10 minutes until thickened. Remove from the heat and allow to cool a little before pouring into the flan case. Leave until cold. Melt the chocolate in a bowl over hot water and stir in the remaining cream. Spread over the filling and chill in the refrigerator for at least 2 hours before serving.

By The Cottage Gate *by Benjamin D. Sigmund*

Hikers Lunch

This is a very old recipe and these filling rolls make a first rate open air meal.

1¼ lb bread dough   1 lb sausages or sausagemeat

Make the bread dough with yeast in the normal way. Set oven to 425°F or Mark 7. Remove the skins from the sausages, if used. Cut off pieces of dough and wrap them around each skinned sausage or the equivalent sausagemeat rolled into sausages. The dough cover should be ¼ to ½ inch thick. Leave to rise in a greased oven tin in a warm place for 20 minutes or until well risen. Bake for 15 minutes and then reduce the temperature to 350° or Mark 4 for a further 20 minutes. Transfer to a wire rack to cool and eat cold.

Cheese and Ham Scones

These are delicious when split and spread with butter or cream cheese.

8 oz self-raising flour	2 oz strong Cheddar cheese, grated
2 teaspoons baking powder	2 oz cooked ham, chopped
Pinch of salt	5 fl oz water
1 oz butter, softened	Beaten egg to glaze

Set oven to 425°F or Mark 7. Grease a baking sheet. Sift the flour, baking powder and salt into a mixing bowl. Rub in the butter until the mixture resembles breadcrumbs and then stir in the grated cheese and chopped ham. Make a well in the centre of the mixture and pour in sufficient of the water to form a soft but not sticky dough. Turn out on to a floured surface and knead lightly until smooth. Roll or pat out to a thickness of $^1/_2$ inch. Cut into 12 rounds with a 2 inch cutter. Gather up the trimmings and use to make a few more scones. Place the scones on the baking sheet and brush each with beaten egg. Bake for 10 to 12 minutes until well risen and golden brown. Transfer to a wire rack to cool.

Waiting for Mother *by Birket Foster*

Chicken, Pork and Herb Pie

This tasty pie is a meal in itself and goes well with a crisp green salad.

1½ lb flour   2 teaspoons salt   4 oz lard   2 oz butter   10 fl oz water
FILLING: 1 lb chicken (breast or thigh meat), sliced   1 lb pork fillet, sliced
1 onion, chopped   ½ teaspoon ground mace   ¼ teaspoon grated nutmeg
1 tablespoon fresh thyme   ½ tablespoon fresh sage leaves, chopped
Salt and pepper   1 egg, beaten   2 teaspoons gelatine
10 fl oz hot chicken stock   3 tablespoons fresh parsley, chopped

Set oven to 400ºF or Mark 6. Grease a deep, 8 inch round cake tin, preferably with a removable base. Sift the flour and salt into a bowl and make a well. Heat the lard, butter and water in a small pan and bring to the boil. Pour into the flour and quickly mix to a soft dough. Turn out on to a floured surface and knead until smooth. Set aside a quarter of the dough and keep covered in a warm place. Use the remaining pastry to line the base and sides of the tin. Layer the chicken and pork in the pastry case, scattering the layers with the herbs and season each layer with salt and pepper. Roll out the reserved pastry and cover the pie, dampening the edges to seal. Decorate with trimmings and cut a steam hole. Brush with beaten egg. Bake for 30 minutes. Brush again with egg, reduce temperature to 325ºF or Mark 3 and bake for another 45 minutes until golden brown. Dissolve the gelatine in the stock, season to taste and, as the pie cools, pour the stock into the hole using a small funnel. Chill overnight.

Cheese and Tomato Bread

A rich, moist savoury loaf that is quick and easy to make.

9 oz self-raising flour	**2 tablespoons tomato purée**
1 teaspoon baking powder	**5 oz strong Cheddar cheese, grated**
4 eggs	**6 sun-dried tomatoes, chopped**
2 tablespoons oil	**1 tablespoon fresh basil leaves, chopped**

Salt and pepper

Set oven to 350°F or Mark 4. Grease and line a 1 lb loaf tin. Sift the flour and baking powder into a mixing bowl. Beat in the eggs, oil and tomato purée. Stir in the rest of the ingredients and season well. Spoon the mixture into the tin, smooth the top and bake for about 45 minutes until the loaf is cooked through and a skewer inserted comes out clean. Turn out on to a wire rack to cool.

Salmon Mousse

This delectable dish brings a touch of sophistication to any al fresco open-air meal.

1 lb fresh salmon	**4 fl oz dry sherry**
Bunch fresh herbs or bouquet garni	**2 tablespoons lemon juice**
$^1/_2$ pint double cream	**Salt and pepper**
2 oz butter	**$^1/_2$ oz powdered gelatine**

Set oven to 350ºF or Mark 4. Lightly oil a 1 lb loaf tin or a salmon mould. Place the salmon in a buttered, ovenproof dish with the fresh herbs and cover with water. Cover the dish with foil and cook for 20 minutes. Leave the salmon to cool in the liquid, then remove the skin and bones, but reserve the liquid. Pound the salmon until smooth. Lightly whip the cream and fold into the salmon. Soften the butter and stir into the mixture together with the sherry and lemon juice. Season to taste. Measure 6 tablespoons of the reserved fish liquid into a bowl and sprinkle the gelatine on top. Set over a pan of hot water until the gelatine has dissolved. Cool slightly and then beat into the mousse. Spoon the mousse into the tin or mould and leave to set in the refrigerator overnight. Serve either turned out on to a serving dish or straight from the tin.

METRIC CONVERSIONS

The weights, measures and oven temperatures used in the preceding recipes can be easily converted to their metric equivalents. The conversions listed below are only approximate, having been rounded up or down as may be appropriate.

Weights

Avoirdupois	Metric
1 oz.	just under 30 grams
4 oz. (¼ lb.)	app. 115 grams
8 oz. (½ lb.)	app. 230 grams
1 lb.	454 grams

Liquid Measures

Imperial	Metric
1 tablespoon (liquid only)	20 millilitres
1 fl. oz.	app. 30 millilitres
1 gill (¼ pt.)	app. 145 millilitres
½ pt.	app. 285 millilitres
1 pt.	app. 570 millilitres
1 qt.	app. 1.140 litres

Oven Temperatures

	°Fahrenheit	Gas Mark	°Celsius
Slow	300	2	150
	325	3	170
Moderate	350	4	180
	375	5	190
	400	6	200
Hot	425	7	220
	450	8	230
	475	9	240

Flour as specified in these recipes refers to plain flour unless otherwise described.